Christian Perspectives
on
Development Issues

Series Editor: Enda McDonagh

FAMINE

Michael Drumm

TRÓCAIRE

Catholic Agency for World Development,
169 Booterstown Avenue,
Blackrock,
Co. Dublin,
Ireland.

Tel: +353 1 288 5385
Fax: +353 1 288 3577
e-mail: info@trocaire.ie
http://www.trocaire.org

VERITAS

Veritas House,
7-8 Lr Abbey Street,
Dublin 1,
Ireland.

Tel: +353 1 878 8177
Fax: +353 1 878 6507
http://www.veritas.ie

CAFOD

Catholic Fund for Overseas Development,
Romero Close,
Stockwell Road,
London SW9 8TY,
U.K.

Tel: +44 171 733 7900
Fax: +44 171 274 9630
e-mail: hqcafod@cafod.org.uk
http://www.cafod.org.uk

© 1998 Michael Drumm

Design/layout: Harrison Design
Printed in Ireland by Genprint

ISBN 1 85390 407 4

Contents

Foreword
Bishop John Kirby, Chairman of Trócaire

Anniversaries are a time for looking back and reviewing what we have accomplished and what remains undone, as well as for looking forward, renewing commitment and rededicating ourselves to the task. On the occasion of Trócaire's 25th anniversary in 1998, we reviewed various aspects of our work overseas and at home.

A major international conference explored the issue of People, Power and Participation and considered civil society in the developing world and its role in protecting, preserving and promoting human rights and democracy. Ten eminent human rights defenders with whom Trócaire has worked in the three continents of the South spoke eloquently of the denial of the most basic rights to millions of the world's citizens. Speakers echoed the words of Pope John Paul II when he said that "A type of development which does not respect and promote human rights is not really worthy of humankind" (*Sollicitudo Rei Socialis, 33*).

The anniversary year has provided an opportunity to focus anew on the Christian inspiration behind the work of Trócaire. The founding documents of Trócaire gave the organisation a very clear mandate and situated this within the work of the Church and within Catholic Social Teaching. Now as we approach the Great Jubilee of the Year 2000 it is timely to revisit some of the major issues that have been central to the work of Trócaire to date and to anticipate the challenges that lie ahead.

Hence, this new joint Trócaire/Veritas series exploring Christian perspectives on key development issues. We are delighted to have our sister development agency in the UK, CAFOD, as co-publisher of the series. We have invited eminent scholars to examine major strands in the work of

Trócaire and to elucidate from a theological perspective the impulses that motivate the practical projects and programmes that Trócaire supports around the developing world. The result is a rich resource of analysis, reflection and restatement of the Christian commitment to solidarity and the oneness of the human family.

I would like to pay tribute to each of the authors for contributing so generously of their talent and their time in the preparation of these Reflections. We owe to our series editor, Professor Enda McDonagh, a profound gratitude for the inspiring guidance he has shown to authors and Trócaire staff engaged in this project. I am confident that the output will be of great practical use to Trócaire in charting its way as well as being of interest to all of those concerned to rise to the challenge of creating a world suffused by the Christian commitment to the dignity of each and every person.

INTRODUCTION
Enda McDonagh, Series Editor

As part of the celebrations of the 25th anniversary of its foundation and more importantly in preparation for its work in the new millennium, Trócaire has begun a fresh examination of its Christian-Catholic roots. With the help of an inter-disciplinary group of advisors and with Veritas and Cafod as co-publishers it has initiated a series of brief, accessible studies under the general title "Christian Perspectives on Development Issues". The aim of these studies is to set in dialogue the rich and varied Christian tradition in teaching and practice of commitment to the poor and excluded with the current concerns of a development agency like Trócaire. In this way it is hoped to enlighten the Christian understanding and renew the spiritual energies of Trócaire, of its staff at home and abroad, and of its supporters and contributors. Without such enlightenment and renewal the vision and work of Trócaire could become narrow and frustrating.

To ensure that such studies are really helpful the particular topics must be carefully chosen in the light of people's needs and Trócaire's commitments. The first titles in the series, *Human Rights*, *Land* and *Famine* illustrate three of the most urgent concerns for Trócaire and other development agencies. In seeking to expose Christian perspectives on these issues, the authors have undertaken a practical theological exploration from biblical background to contemporary analysis. While maintaining close communication with concrete problems of the day they have drawn on developing Christian tradition to illuminate and deepen commitment to justice in the world, that commitment element of the Gospel as the 1971 Synod of Bishops called it.

The series is designed not only to enhance the understanding and motivation of development agencies and workers; the studies themselves make clear how much theology has to learn from work in the field, how much theory has to gain from praxis. In fact the social encyclicals which form the basis of so much social thought and activity in the Church were themselves influenced at various times by practical developments as individual Church people and organisations reached out to the needy and excluded. In an increasingly pragmatic culture, the witness of Christian practice can be an effective way of understanding and expressing the presence of God. To do justice, the prophet Jeremiah says, is to know God. Engagement with the task of promoting a truly just world is for Christians a response to the call of the Reign or Kingdom of God. In the doing comes the understanding. Theologians need to learn by doing also and by being actively associated with the doers and seekers of justice, freedom, truth and peace. Studies such as these will, it is hoped, prove of help to religious thinkers who have not as yet had the opportunity for more active involvement in justice issues. Being drawn into that work their insights into the whole range of Christian doctrine and practice from the Trinity, Incarnation and the last things to environmental protection will be undoubtedly enriched. Out of that enrichment they will contribute in turn to the Christian perspectives on development work which Trócaire is in search of here.

Multiple challenges remain. There is a whole range of particular topics and of refinements of these topics from poverty to gender, to race, to environment which demand parallel treatment to the benefit of Trócaire's work and to the benefit of theology itself. Several of these studies will be undertaken in the run up to the millennium.

There are dangers also. There is the danger that such studies might become too self-enclosing or too bland or too negatively disputatious. With a good advisory team these particular dangers can be averted. So can the more subtle one whereby the work of a development agency of explicit

Christian-Catholic inspiration is perceived as and/or becomes a vehicle for religious conversion. Trócaire and similar agencies have, true to their mandate and to their genuine Christian inspiration, respected these distinctions very scrupulously. It would be very sad if its attempt to explore its theological roots were to obscure rather than clarify its integrity as a development agency devoted fully to the personal and social needs of the people they serve without any threat to the cultural or religious integrity of these people. It will therefore be a matter of real concern for the editor and authors of these studies to ensure that the renewal of Christian understanding and inspiration further protects and deepens the integrity of Trócaire and its work. In that also they will be making a further contribution to maintaining the varied vocation and work of the whole Church in the modern world.

Executive Summary

This paper is a reflection on the reality of famine from a perspective that is both Christian and Irish. It begins with an analysis of Ireland's Great Hunger of the 1840s and the enduring legacy of that catastrophe. The author argues that it is only in recent times that we have begun to come to terms with the memory and consequences of what was probably the most important event in Irish history. Reflection on this experience raises many significant issues that might contribute to the continuing debate on famine.

Chapter Two comments on various responses to famine. Particular attention is focused on the question of aid. It is argued that relief aid can be beneficial but that in and of itself it is of limited value. Attention must also be paid to the realities of poverty and war which are often the real causes of famine. As a result those who seek to relieve the pain caused by famine must address the political and economic structures which allow famines to continue in a world with plenty of food for everyone.

All of these issues raise important questions for Christian faith. The origins of Christianity are found in Jesus' preaching of the reign of God almost two thousand years ago. The task of Christian discipleship is to follow in the footsteps of Jesus. This demands that his ministry of bringing healing and hope into a broken world must be continued. Chapter Three raises questions that Christians need to reflect upon as they seek to proclaim God's kingdom in our world today.

The study closes with some comments on the eucharist. Given that bread is the central symbol of Christian faith and the breaking of bread is its core ritual, the reality of spiritual and physical hunger should never be far from our minds. As in the Eucharist bread and wine become the body and blood of Christ so Christians are called to work with all people of good will to transform our world. In the case of famine this will demand that we muster all the intellectual and moral energy at our disposal to address what remains one of the greatest scandals of our time.

CHAPTER 1

The Irish Experience of Famine[1]

The sufferings of our unhappy people are beyond description. Every hour the calamity is increasing. Coroner's Inquests have ceased to afford anything like a true account of the misery which prevails because hundreds of unfortunate creatures have, within the last week, died of starvation, upon whom no inquests were held. They were hurried to the grave coffinless and shroudless, so great is the mortality that the ancient customs are forgotten and we now see no such thing as a well attended funeral.

The Sligo Champion, 26 February 1847

Famine is always obscene. But the obscenity deserves serious reflection. To explain, excuse, eclipse or empty famine of its horror, its causes or its consequences on the basis of belief in God is scandalous. In the case of famine, God is not available as an easy answer to our problems. The goal of this paper is not to explain the immediate causes of famine - this is a task better undertaken by historians, economists, nutritionists and agricultural scientists - but to analyse the impact of famine on our religious sensibilities and the challenges it poses to Christian belief and responsibility. Such analysis will inevitably raise questions associated with the moral causes and implications of famine. Initially we will turn our attention to the Irish famine of the 1840s and then we will study how theological reflection on the reality of famine might contribute to the educational and development work of an organisation like Trócaire.

---

1 Some of the material used in this paper has been published in "Irish Catholics: A people formed by ritual" in Eoin G. Cassidy ed., *Faith and Culture in the Irish Context*, Dublin, Veritas, 1996, pp. 83-99, and in M. Drumm, *Passage to Pasch*, Dublin, Columba Press, 1998.

The Great Hunger of the 1840s

The experience of hunger has echoed throughout history. At different times famines have decimated various regions and nations but in the modern era few countries have been ravished by the effects of famine as Ireland was. In terms of the number of deaths, (the well-known famines of the 1970s in Bangladesh, the Sahel and Ethiopia killed far fewer whilst the much more destructive famines in Stalin's Ukraine in the 1930s, Bengal in the 1940s and as part of China's Great Leap Forward in the 1950s took place amongst populations far greater than Ireland's), the absence of war, (unlike Biafra in the 1970s, Ethiopia in the 1980s and Somalia and Sudan in the 1990s), and its duration over five to six years (when most famines last from six months to two years, only the Bengali Famine of the 1940s continued for so long), the Irish famine of the 1840s was one of the greatest disasters in the peacetime history of the world.[2] Not surprisingly it came to be known as the Great Hunger. It is difficult to overstate the horror that unfolded. Statistics are always bland and cold; one must remember that behind each statistic stands a human person. The population of the island fell from approximately 8.5 millions in 1846 to about 6.5 millions in 1851. The census of 1841 measured the Irish population as 8,175,125; in 1851 it was 6,552,385. But the population was rising in the early 1840s and had probably reached 8.5 millions by 1846. At least one million people died and even more than that emigrated. The worst affected region was the province of Connacht, (counties Galway, Leitrim, Mayo, Roscommon and Sligo), where in five years the population dropped by one third. The population of Connacht in 1841 was 1,418,859; in 1851 it had dropped to 1,010,031. As in the rest of the country the population was rising in the early 1840s and had probably

---

2 See Cormac O Grada, "The Great Famine and Today's Famines", in Cathal Poirteir ed., *The Great Irish Famine*, Cork, Mercier Press 1995, pp. 248-258.

TRÓCAIRE/VERITAS/CAFOD

reached 1.5 millions by 1846. This was a disaster on a scale seldom, if ever, encountered before. Over a short few years the world of Irish cottiers and farm labourers ruptured and died.

There is much to be learned from reflection upon these events and their aftermath. It has taken 150 years to come to terms with many of the relevant issues. It is interesting to note that the 150th anniversary of the Great Hunger coincides with the twenty-fifth anniversary of the establishment of Trócaire, the Irish Catholic Church's agency charged with long-term development aid, emergency relief and prophetic education. This is a happy coincidence since Trócaire and the Irish Catholic Church in general need look no further than Ireland's modern history to learn much about the reality of famine. Given the enormity of the forces unleashed in Ireland in the middle of the nineteenth century one should be slow to underestimate their effects on the consciousness of Irish Catholics. I would like to look briefly at four such effects.

1. Suppressing the memory

One of the key insights of contemporary psychology is that people suppress the memory of great traumas in their individual lives. Similarly Irish people suppressed the memory of the Great Hunger. When one begins to delve into the tragedy of the horror that unfolded this is easy to understand. In the aftermath of famine there are no good stories to tell; rather the chances are that the main stories are of neglect, cheating, stealing, gaining on the backs of others and the ultimate horror - cannibalism. This is not the stuff of songs and fireside storytelling. In famine it is impossible to identify the enemy and so heroism is difficult to describe: it is easy enough to identify and laud the hero in the face of colonial occupation but what is heroism in the face of famine? Who were the heroes - those who died? Those who emigrated? Those who survived at home?

The latter group gained as a result of the famine and one can legitimately speak of a survivor complex. It seems almost too obvious to remark upon but it is worth reflecting on the fact that the people who now live in Ireland are the descendants of those who survived the horror of famine; the majority of their forebears did not die or emigrate. In reality the gains in the medium term for those who survived were very significant economically, socially and politically. It seems plausible to surmise that they might indeed repress the memory of the Great Hunger and in this their behaviour is clearly distinct from the Irish of the diaspora. Folklore traditions amongst the native Irish relating to the famine are scarce whereas the famine remained one of the great themes in the lives of the Irish of the diaspora. Here's a simple example: ask Irish Catholics living in Ireland to analyse the historical causes of the troubles since 1969 and they will speak of plantations and Cromwell. Ask the same question in Irish Catholic working-class areas of Liverpool or Boston and one will almost invariably hear of the famine. The ultimate demonstration of suppressing the memory was the centenary years of 1945-48 when the neophyte state all but ignored the events of one hundred years earlier.

Why do we now recall the famine one hundred and fifty years later? As ever historical distance has opened up more space to reflect. Poets,[3] dramatists[4] and historians have given us language, images and analysis to think through the horror. Missionaries and aid workers have encountered famine anew and their contemporary experience has retrieved a long lost memory in the Irish psyche. It is imperative that we, the descendants of the survivors, now re-member what happened. The best way to do so is through ritual which allows us to

3 Patrick Kavanagh's poem *The Great Hunger* is still probably the most famous poetic contribution; more recently see Desmond Egan, *In the Holocaust of Autumn*, Newbridge, Co. Kildare, the Goldsmith Press, 1994.
4 Tom Murphy, *Famine*, was first performed in the Peacock Theatre, Dublin in 1968. His own comments on the drama are notable, see T. Murphy, *Plays: One*, London, Methuen Drama, 1993, pp. ix-xvii.

celebrate rather than just study the past. Imagine the significance of a small community gathering to honour an unmarked mass grave, to admit the pain of history, to pray for responsible leadership, to hope for justice and to lay to rest finally those who died such terrible deaths. We need to remember so that we can legitimately forget. There are places in the land and places in the soul where we can re-member; having visited these places we can - indeed we probably must - legitimately forget.

2. Surviving the consequences

People and institutions adapt and change in the midst of overwhelming catastrophe. The Irish Catholic Church was rocked to its very core by the events of the 1840s and not least by the widely held belief that Anglicans and Presbyterians had used the tragedy for their own purposes. The Catholic Church under Archbishop Paul Cullen's leadership and with the outstanding contribution of the new religious orders responded aggressively. Education and health care provision became key pastoral goals in Irish Catholic communities throughout the world as people sought to protect themselves against future horrors. Irish Catholics began to build - churches, presbyteries, hospitals, schools. For a people bereft of buildings for centuries these new constructions became an important symbol of their faith and even down to today one will hear the complaint that Irish clergy are preoccupied with church buildings to the neglect of more immediate pastoral issues. But one should not dismiss lightly the psychological importance of these new buildings that sprouted up all over the country in the latter part of the last century; at least one Catholic would live in a house to vie with the local landlord, and so the parish priest's house was a rather large construction for a single, celibate man.

The consequences of the famine were evident in all spheres of Irish life but probably nowhere more clearly than in attitudes towards sexuality. After the famine people feared what the future might hold, not least for their children, and consequently they married later in life and many never married at all. The Catholic Church preached a message of temperance and sexual abstinence and the newly emerging Catholic middle-class rejected the raucous religious expression of an earlier age in the embrace of personal scrupulosity, individual ambition and religious rigour. The latter was facilitated by frequent recourse to the sacrament of confession whilst the dominance of Victorian values in a wider context reinforced an atmosphere of sexual repression. In the aftermath of terrible famine it is not difficult to link sexual expression and guilt; celibacy and sexual abstinence would have emerged as socio-economic as well as religious values. Sexual experience and guilt feelings appear to be linked in manifold different ways but one must surely regret the oppressive ethos of sexual repression so characteristic of post-famine Irish life.

3. Characterising relationships

Relationships between Irish Catholics and Protestants have always been fraught with difficulty but probably hit their lowest ebb in the immediate aftermath of the famine. There have been sectarian riots on the streets of Belfast in every decade since the 1840s. Accusations of proselytism poisoned relationships in many local communities and it is only since the 1960s that a real dialogue has commenced. Relationships between Anglicans and Catholics deteriorated noticeably from the 1820s onwards: Catholics in Ireland believed that a new proselytising zeal was evident amongst Anglican evangelicals whilst a resurgent Catholicism in England sowed fear in the hearts of many Irish Protestants. Suggestions of cultural superiority were common amongst Protestant commentators. Yet what was really significant was the perceived effort to convert the Irish poor through what came to be known as the "New Reformation."[5]

These tensions ultimately found their focus in the famine controversy over "souperism", the claim that Anglican evangelicals distributed soup to impoverished Catholics on condition that they converted to Anglicanism and sent their children to what was effectively the equivalent of Sunday School. People who "took the soup" became known as "soupers" and later Irish Catholic tradition used this term to identify those who had apostasised and to highlight the great Catholic triumph in convincing most adherents not to "take the soup". That a significant number of Anglican evangelicals indulged in this grotesque form of proselytism is unquestionably true; that many Irish Anglican pastors abhorred the practice is equally true.[6] The guilty included Thomas Plunkett, Bishop of the united dioceses of Tuam, Killala and Achonry, Alexander R.C. Dallas, founder of the Society for Irish Church Missions and Edward Nangle who set up a Protestant colony in Achill. Their actions, particularly in County Mayo, were abhorrent and were well summarised by Dallas himself when he wrote that his movement "was nurtured in blood". He added that:

> ...the awful famine of 1847, with its attendant horrors in 1848 worked wonderfully for its development. Thus it might almost be said that the movement gave a character to the famine rather than the famine characterised the movement.[7]

---

5 See Donal A. Kerr, 'A Nation of Beggars'? Priests, people and politics in Famine Ireland 1846-52, Oxford, Clarendon Press 1994, pp. 206 and 324.
6 These issues are analysed in two works by Desmond Bowen, Souperism: Myth or Reality, A study of Catholics and Protestants during the Great Famine, Cork, Mercier Press, 1970 and The Protestant Crusade in Ireland 1800-70, Dublin, Gill and Macmillan, 1978. For a very different perspective on the reality of "souperism" see, Irene Whelan, "The Stigma of Souperism" in Cathal Porteir, op, cit., pp. 135-154.
7 Quoted in Desmond Bowen, Souperism: Myth or Reality, op.cit., p. 127.

Understandably Catholic leaders responded aggressively to what they perceived to be a second Reformation; Tobias Kirby, the Vice-Rector of the Irish College in Rome, advised the bishops "to repress any efforts of the Protestants who give the poor a morsel of bread with one hand and kill their immortal souls with the other".[8] As before, a Reformation would be met head on with a Counter-Reformation. The leader of this Counter-Reformation was Archbishop Paul Cullen. It was undoubtedly true that "for Cullen, countering Protestant proselytism was a priority and his hatred of it is crucial to an understanding of his policy in his early years in Ireland".[9] But Cullen was not the only one who was horrified at what some Anglican evangelicals were attempting to do. It is not an exaggeration to say that the controversy over soup made an almost indelible psychological mark on later Irish Catholics both at home and abroad. The fact that some proselytisers actually used the horrible situation in which so many people found themselves to further their own goals was unquestionably obscene. Ironically it galvanised the Irish Catholic Church to provide education and health care on a vast scale and this in turn facilitated the emergence of the Catholic middle-class that led the struggle for land reform and ultimately for national independence. But the bitter memory remained of a people who were threatened with the robbery of their culture and traditions because they were hungry. This memory left its mark on the Irish Catholic psyche in general and not least on the leadership of the Church.

There is deep suspicion between the Christian communities in Ireland over land, nationality and colonialism; the wounds of history are deep. The imagination still bears the scars of the famine that was endured, the land that was fought over and the language that was suppressed. Famine, land, language - could you think of greater forces for forming the imagination?

8 Quoted in Desmond Bowen, *Souperism: Myth or Reality*, op.cit., p. 143
9 Donal A. Kerr, p. 324, op. cit.

It is hardly surprising that feelings of inferiority, peasantry and pain are so much a part of Irish Catholic consciousness. The great danger with an inferiority complex is that it withdraws into a ghetto smugly secure with its own certainties concerning the hostile world outside. Unquestionably Irish Catholicism gave way to this temptation so that as late as the 1950s one finds the best minds of the Irish Catholic Church dealing with questions such as attendance at services in Protestant churches, state regulations concerning dances and the endless minutiae of liturgical rubrics.[10] This was a Church utterly preoccupied with its relationship to Protestantism.

But there is another relationship that might prove even more important in the longer run - the relationship of Irish Catholics to the enlightenment consciousness of the modern world. The conventional wisdom of the liberal media/academic establishment in contemporary Ireland is that Irish Catholics were held in bondage for centuries by an oppressive Church and that only with open access to education since the 1960s have people begun to escape the clutches of this all powerful institution. I believe this form of analysis to be fundamentally flawed. As a simple hypothesis that explains everything that needs to be explained it is very attractive but such all-embracing hypotheses are invariably false. What alternative explanation might one offer? We have failed to give sufficient weight to the effect of the Great Hunger of the 1840s on Irish Catholic consciousness. Instead of the rights of the individual, freedom of enquiry, respect for the emerging sciences and progress, the famine turned the hearts and minds of Irish Catholics in a different direction - towards survival, tenant rights, emigration and fear of what life might hold. It took generations to come to terms with these issues. As a result there is an extraordinary coincidence in Ireland in the 1960s of

---

10 These and other examples can be found in the pages of the *Irish Ecclesiastical Record,* a review which gives an interesting insight into clerical preoccupations since the famine.

modernity (in terms of the beginning of industrialisation, urbanisation and secularisation) with the Second Vatican Council. Just as modernity was beginning to doubt its own values both Ireland and the Catholic Church were embracing it for the first time. For Irish Catholics it was a time of overwhelming change; there was the crucial call to inculturate the faith in a truly modern way so that believers could articulate their faith for a newly emerging world.[11] This must remain the key pastoral priority for the Irish Catholic Church. But if one ignores the historical experience of famine in Ireland then one is likely to draw many mistaken conclusions about the nature of Irish Catholicism.

4. Inculturating the Christian faith in Ireland - yesterday and today

The inter-relationship of faith and culture is, from a theological perspective, an issue of inculturation, of how one articulates and incarnates Christian belief in a particular culture. In an Irish context one must remember that the dialogue of faith and culture goes back about 1,500 years and that it endured one of the great peace-time calamities in the middle of the last century. One should not reduce this dialogue to simply a matter of how Irish Catholicism might interact with the enlightenment. Rather we might bring forth many riches from our past to help us incarnate the faith in a post-modern context. We could look again at the emphasis on communal rituals rather than just the individual subject's search for meaning; at the interaction of Christian and pagan motifs; at the celebration of the earth; at the encounter with mystery and otherness in many of our traditions. This is already happening in what is termed Celtic Spirituality but one should be aware

---

11 This call is well expressed by Dermot Lane in 'Faith and Culture: the Challenge of Inculturation', in Dermot Lane ed., *Religion and Culture in Dialogue*, Dublin, Columba Press, 1993, pp. 11-39.

that this spirituality is filtered through the historical experience of Irish Catholics; there is no ahistorical access to such a spirituality.

The spirituality of poor Irish Catholics in pre-famine times revolved around blessings and wakes, fasting and pilgrimage, station masses and rosaries. This was a traditional religion. When I refer to traditional religion I mean that matrix of beliefs, practices, rituals and customs that constitutes a living incarnate religion. Such a religion functions in a very practical way as an interpretative model of human existence and brings together in an apparently unholy alliance the residue of archaic fertility rites, land based rituals, orthodox Christian beliefs and a broad notion of the sacramentality of life. There is much in the traditional practices of Irish Catholics that has not been integrated into any coherent theological framework; just think of fairy forts, holy wells, bonfire nights, ghost stories, pilgrimages, patterns, wakes. All of the latter have constituted rich data for folklorists, artists and anthropologists but have been largely ignored by theologians probably because it was the pastoral policy of the Church to try and banish many of these traditions. Donal Kerr comments:

> The cluster of beliefs and practices that constituted the religion of the poorer peasants, in addition to such central Catholic devotions as the sacraments, the rosary, fasting and daily prayers, also included devotions connected with patterns, pilgrimages, holy wells, wakes and charms. Many of these came under attack, as a reforming Church opposed them as either superstitious or providing the occasion for insobriety, immorality, or other abuses. The Famine dealt them a devastating blow, for it bore heaviest on the labouring and cottier classes. Thenceforth, religious practices became more "orthodox" and the quickening pace at which this took place wrought a rapid change in Irish devotional life.[12]

12 Donal A. Kerr, pp. 318-19, op. cit.

And yet the change was not complete, the exorcism failed to banish all the ancient archetypes. Despite the unleashing of massive iconoclastic forces in the midst of a society in disarray, where death and emigration stalked the land and the language of the people faced near terminal decline, this effort to redefine the boundaries of human community by banishing so many traditions could not ultimately succeed as it failed to give due weight to the imagination and its capacity to revisit these ancient wellsprings.

As today we attempt to decipher our past we must be careful not to dismiss the religious experience of our forebears as little more than superstition or empty ritualism. A poor and broken people are always iconophile for they have little to hold on to and even less to explain what is happening. The iconoclasm of the well-fed stomach should at least hesitate in its theological judgements. Hunger stalked the land of Ireland many times in the 19th century; most shockingly of all it revisited the people of Connacht thirty years after the Great Hunger in the late 1870s. In 1879 the poor of Mayo were in a wretched state and on 21 August, several people claimed to see a Marian apparition on the gable wall of the church in Knock. Michael Davitt's land war was about to begin and the word "boycott" would soon enter the English language. Yet again the complex iconography of the Irish was expressing itself.

Great historical forces have shaped the religious consciousness of Irish Catholics. Over the centuries Christian and pagan rituals formed a vibrant pre-modern expression of religious belief. The Great Hunger of the 1840s and the forces that it unleashed gave a particular flavour to Irish Catholicism. Only since the 1960s has this pre-modern mix of faith and culture hit the rocks of modernity. Naturally this has given rise to a certain shapelessness as the icons of an earlier time came under sustained critique. Different groups and individuals will respond in varied ways to this critique, but as we move beyond the innocence of an earlier time and the reductionistic certainties of modernity, a new post-modern era of uncertainty and otherness lies ahead of us. In determining new shapes for the Irish Catholicism of the future we will inevitably have to face the reality of the past. An organisation like Trócaire has an important role to play in shaping the Irish Catholic Church of the future. The Irish bishops request Trócaire to respond to the reality of famine on three distinct levels:

through the provision of emergency relief to meet immediate practical needs for food, medicine and shelter; through long-term development projects aimed at the rebuilding of local communities through agriculture, health and education programmes; through its prophetic advocacy of the cause of the suffering people by criticising publicly the political and economic structures which lead to the catastrophe.[13]

It is probably true to say that the famine relief work of Irish non-governmental agencies disturbed the repressed memory of famine in the Irish soul. Even in the limited reflections of this paper one can see how significant this might turn out to be.

One of the most important results of the Great Hunger was an extraordinary dedication to the provision of education and health care as people sought to protect themselves against future disasters. The Church responded through contributing enormous resources of personnel for education and health care provision. For one hundred years after the Great Hunger these personnel were drawn in the main from the ranks of religious orders. Today the Church must turn to its lay membership to take up this task in order to forge a relevant response to the reality of famine. As the state properly takes over the financing of social services it is the responsibility of the Christian community to turn its attention to those most in need

---

13 Pastoral Letter of the Bishops of Ireland on the Occasion of Famine Remembrance Sunday, September 24, 1995. See *Intercom*, October 1995, p. 21.

both at home and abroad. Through development aid, crisis relief and a prophetic voice in politics and education Trócaire is well placed to provide an important outreach for the Irish Church. To inculturate the gospel today will surely mean addressing the realities of grinding poverty, human rights abuses and social exclusion. In contributing to such inculturation Trócaire will be providing a critical dimension to the life of the Christian community in Ireland and overseas.

CHAPTER 2

Theological Interpretations of Famine

Given the significance of famines in human history one finds many different theological interpretations of their causes, their meaning and their implications for Christian belief and action. In this paper we will focus on three central issues in Christian theology: 1. responding to the reality of famine; 2. proclaiming the reign of God; 3. celebrating the eucharist. We will continue to make reference to the Great Hunger of the 1840s for it provides a link between the reality of famine in our own history and the work of Trócaire today.

Responding to the reality of famine

As ever our bias and prejudice tells us more about ourselves than we care to admit. When I began reading Irish homilies and episcopal statements from the 1840s I expected to find expressions of divine retribution, the justice of God, the rights of property, the comforting of the afflicted and the call to follow Christ with a humble, contrite spirit on the way to Calvary. But my bias and prejudice were wrong. Instead I found a vehement rejection of appeals to divine retribution, an appeal for human justice, an objection to the abuse of the rights of property, a demand that the consciences of the comfortable be afflicted and an acknowledgement that though one must try in faith to understand all human suffering as part of the mystery of Christ one must do everything in one's power to put an end to this horror. The theological comments of those who lived through great human disasters are always more enlightening that the cosy conclusions of later writers. Let's listen to the contemporary voice of the 1840s.

The 1847 annual meeting of the Catholic bishops was held in Dublin in October. The meeting took place a month earlier than usual because of the terrible conditions in the country.

This was "Black '47" and the people faced a winter of interminable suffering. The bishops sought and were granted a meeting with Lord Clarendon, the Lord Lieutenant. In their address to him they attacked the penal laws as the long-term cause of the famine. They spoke of "the unjust penal enactments which, in other days, deprived the great bulk of the people of the rights of property, thus discouraging industry by debarring them from the enjoyment of its fruits".[14] They rejected the suggestion that the laziness and backwardness of the people were to blame for the terrible famine:

> It is in the violation of the principle of justice and of Christian morality from which those enactments had sprung and not to any innate indolence of the people that we may trace their depressed social condition, which, sinking gradually into still greater misery, terminated last year, by the failure of the potatoe crop, in the famine so tremendous in its havoc, and of which the present season threatens the appalling recurrence.[15]

One of the other great themes of the 1840s concerned the rights of property. Landlords surely had a right to an income from their holdings which would justify further investment and enhance productivity. The large number of tenants inhibited such developments. The bishops commented: "Hallowed as are the rights of property, those of life are still more sacred, and rank as such in every well regulated scale that adjusts the relative possessions of man."[16]

Laws which protect the rights of property whilst ignoring the rights of life are condemned:

---

14 *Catholic Directory 1848*, pp. 238-39.
15 Ibid. p. 239.
16 Ibid. p. 239.

Yet laws sanctioning such unnatural injustice, and, therefore, injurious to society, not only exist but are extensively enforced with reckless and unrelenting rigour, while the sacred and indefeasible rights of life are forgotten amidst the incessant reclamations of the subordinate rights of property.[17]

Given the reality that faced the people it was likely that some would turn to violence. The bishops acknowledged this temptation and in order to overcome it they sought to "procure measures of relief commensurate with the magnitude of the calamity".[18] And then in a very interesting final paragraph they outline a programme of relief that is as relevant today as it was 150 years ago. Rejecting a model of gratuitous charity as abusive and demeaning they leave it to the expertise of the government to determine the precise nature of relief while remarking that

an equitable arrangement of the relations between landlords and tenants, founded on commutative justice, appears to them [the bishops] so necessary, that without it they despair of seeing the poor sufficiently employed and protected, and the land sufficiently cultivated, or the peace and prosperity of the country placed on a secure foundation. Large tracts of land capable of cultivation are now lying waste; the coasts abound in fish, which would give a large supply of food; encouragement to work those and other mines of wealth with which the country is teeming, would be well worthy of the solicitude of her Majesty's government.[19]

---

17 *Catholic Directory 1848*, p. 239.
18 Ibid, p. 240.
19 Ibid, pp. 240-1.

It is clear then that at their meeting in October 1847 the Irish bishops' theological interpretation of the frightful famine unfolding in their dioceses was not one of divine retribution or of economic and social failure on the part of their people but of the responsibilities of government and landowners and the need for relief that would empower the poor to take some hold of their own destiny. This latter point is particularly significant. The bishops were obviously convinced that properly focused relief could have an effect well beyond what the monetary calculation would imply. No doubt they had been encouraged in this by the words of the Bishop of Rome. Earlier that same year Pius IX, only nine months after his election as Pope, had issued an encyclical letter to all the bishops of the world alerting them to the unfolding tragedy in Ireland and reminding them that to come to the assistance of those in great need is at the very heart of their episcopal ministry.[20] He went on:

But we have lately received, and daily still receive, such letters and accounts from Ireland, not only announcing the continuance of these calamities, but their frightful and alarming increase, that our heart has been afflicted with unspeakable grief and our exertions imperatively called for, again to afford them assistance.[21]

The Pope requested prayers and alms-giving for the people of Ireland.

We recommend, that in the dioceses or districts under your control, you should appoint three days for public prayers... At the same time we recommend you, Venerable Brethren, to exercise your charity in exhorting your several flocks to contribute towards the relief of the Irish people.[22]

---

20 The text can be found in the *Catholic Directory 1848*, pp. 205-208.
21 Ibid., p. 206.
22 Ibid.

A further contemporary theological analysis of the famine is to be found in the statement of the Irish bishops at the end of their national synod in Thurles in 1850.[23] They did not mince their words. A failure to expose the reality that had unfolded in the last few years would, they said, amount to "criminal silence" and "criminal neglect".[24] They condemned what had happened in these words:

We behold our poor not only crushed and overwhelmed by the awful visitations of Heaven, but frequently the victims of the most ruthless oppression that ever disgraced the annals of humanity. Though they have been made to the image of the living God, and are purchased by the blood of calvary, - though the special favourites and representatives of Jesus Christ, - we see them treated with a cruelty which would cause the heart to ache if inflicted on the beasts of the field, and for which it would be difficult to find a parallel save in the atrocities of savage life. The desolating track of the exterminator is to be traced in too many parts of the country - in those levelled cottages and roofless abodes, whence so many virtuous and industrious families have been torn by brute force, without distinction of age or sex, sickness or health, and flung upon the highway to perish in the extremity of want.[25]

Echoing some of the words from their address to Lord Clarendon they identified the root cause of the problem as follows:

One of the worst fruits of the False Teaching of the age, has been to generate a spirit of contempt, hard-

---

23 The text was published in the *Catholic Directory 1851*, pp. 184-200.
24 *Catholic Directory 1851*, p. 196.
25 Ibid.

heartedness, and hostility to the Poor. The Mammon of Iniquity, not the Spirit of Christianity, and the avarice which the apostle denounces as the root of all evil, not the charity of Jesus Christ, have furnished the principles and maxims by which they have been estimated and ranked in the social scale.[26]

The severity of these criticisms stung the governing establishment. The Prime Minister, Lord John Russell, said that "no language was omitted which could excite the feelings of the peasant class against those who were owners of the land".[27] Lord Clarendon, in a letter to Russell, condemned the bishops' address as a mixture of medieval bigotry, socialist doctrine and devilish misquotation of scripture which used the mask of religion "to stir up different classes against each other".[28] The facts of the case were very different. The bishops were not bigots nor were they attempting to foment class struggle or to misquote the scriptures, but they were drawing attention to gross violations of the right to life and abuses of the rights of property. They were also insisting that the state is morally obliged to intervene to alleviate suffering on such a huge scale and that those with resources to spare must contribute to the relief of those most in need. In so doing they were attacked with the same cheap slogans to which the rich and powerful have consistently resorted in the last two centuries when serious moral questions are raised concerning the social, political and economic structuring of society. This was the era of *laissez-faire*, a doctrine which in its abject failure to recognise any social vision except that of economic liberalism was and is, from a Christian perspective, utterly reprehensible. In rejecting such an understanding in 1850 the bishops were proposing a different vision based on structural reforms and

---

26 *Catholic Directory 1851*, p. 197.
27 See Donal A. Kerry, op. cit., p. 262.
28 Ibid., p. 231.

immediate relief for those in dire need. In pursuit of the latter they said:

> Surely if ever there was a people whose manifold miseries and privations could pierce the heart of charity to its core, and call for her most devoted exertions and sacrifices, our suffering countrymen at the present hour are pre-eminently entitled to that afflicting distinction. Let your contributions and exertions then, dearly beloved, be proportionate to the wants and calamities you have to succour or alleviate. Enlarge your hearts with the greatness of the occasion which presents itself to you.[29]

The answer to the question of how to respond to famine is never easy but the reality remains that human action or inaction is critical. What the Irish bishops had to say in the midst of the Great Hunger demands respect and reflection. These varied responses to the terrible calamities of the 1840s are mirrored in the decision of the Irish Episcopal Conference to establish Trócaire in 1973. As their predecessors had demanded serious social and economic reforms alongside famine relief almost one hundred and fifty years earlier, so the bishops of the 1970s embarked on a similar agenda for their own times. For the question of responsibility in the face of famine will not go away. The maturity of the response of the bishops to the trauma of the Great Hunger is enlightening even today. One might summarise it in four principles: (i) gratuitous relief can be demeaning and demoralising; (ii) properly focused relief can be very effective in achieving limited goals; (iii) the value of all famine relief is undermined unless it is accompanied by structural reforms which address the long-term causes of famine; (iv) aid intended for the relief of famine should never be used to challenge religious and/or cultural

---

29 *Catholic Directory 1851*, p. 195.

traditions. These principles imply that Christians should not simply throw money at problems, that they should question and reflect upon the nature and motives of various relief agencies and movements, that they should challenge the moral behaviour of governments and non-governmental agencies who demean the humanity and independence of the recipients of aid, that they should contribute willingly and substantially to organisations which seek to alleviate the worst effects of famines whilst empowering the victims to take some hold of their own destiny through giving proper attention to education and planning; that they should seek to become educated concerning the structural causes of famine and social exclusion; that they should be politically active in addressing these issues; that they should never link financial aid with adherence to a particular religious tradition.

Famine in the contemporary world

Principles such as these are valid even today, and may be used to inform the work of Trócaire and other agencies as they attempt to deal responsibly with the reality of hunger in the contemporary world. If one applies these principles to recent famines such as the Ethiopian and Somali famines of the 1980s and early 1990s, as well as the famine that is at present raging in Southern Sudan, then the following lessons emerge.

(i) Gratuitous relief is demeaning for both the giver and the recipient. Learning how to give and how to receive is one of the great achievements of human life both at a personal and communal level. One can give in such a way that alienates the recipient and does nothing more than silence one's conscience or one can enter a relationship which is mutually enriching and truly informs one's conscience. Throwing money at those who are suffering in Southern Sudan or elsewhere ultimately solves nothing. What is required is a relationship in which everyone learns how to give and to receive. In such a relationship, the dignity of those who are impoverished is enhanced and those with plenty can come to appreciate that the poor are not afflicted due to their own inadequacies or failings.

In the world in which we live famine is an economic and political reality which demands a long-term economic and political response. Food aid looks good on television but separated from searching economic, political and social analyses it can amount, at best, to a temporary stopgap which does nothing to address the deeper issues involved, and at worst to a tacit support for tyrannical regimes. A former Sudanese government minister, Bona Malwal, has criticised the international community's response to the current food crisis in his homeland saying that

> they are treating the famine situation in Sudan as if it is different from the current civil conflict and the political crisis in the country. The truth of the matter is that the famine is a man-made catastrophe, manipulated by the regime as a weapon in its treatment of the people in the marginalised areas of Sudan.

The Christian God awaits the human response; God does not force our hand. That the human response often, even normally, fails to materialise from Calvary to Sudan is tragic, that the Christian God ceaselessly prods our conscience to open our eyes to the realities of the world is our hope.

(ii) There is little doubt that focused limited emergency relief can produce beneficial results. Aid agencies have become adept at assessing the needs and, more importantly, the capabilites of vulnerable people. In building long-term relationships of mutual respect and friendship with local communities, agencies can work to reduce peoples' vulnerability to crises. Such vulnerabilities include a shortage of resources, limited income or production opportunities, and internal conflicts amongst many others. However, all communities have some capacity to help themselves and in times of crisis it is these capabilities which should be harnessed in the provision of relief. In times of famine people may be left with very few material possessions, but they will often maintain valuable assets such as leadership, decision-making structures, community and family ties and the motivation to rebuild their lives. While peoples' vulnerabilities will be more obvious in times of disaster, by seeking and utilising their capabilites relief programmes can become more effective in their immediate goals and also facilitate greater involvement of people in their own long-term development.

This would also help agencies to avoid a "messiah complex", the temptation to believe that an organisation can just appear on the scene when an emergency arises and sort out problems that have arisen over many years. The problem with emergency relief is that it can become a pawn in the power struggles of vested interests. In the case of Operation Lifeline Sudan set up in 1989 to ensure access for humanitarian assistance, aid can only be provided to areas approved by the Khartoum government. This clearly gives the government enormous power as controlling the supply of food is one of the most powerful weapons in the Sudanese conflict. That is why those who wish to deal with famine must address the real causes of the horror rather than just bandaging the gaping wound or worse still fuelling the war.

(iii) The key causes of food insecurity and famine over the past thirty years have been poverty and war. "In any food crisis, whether local or large scale, it is the poor who starve." History has shown that periods of severe hunger occur only in those countries whose economies are too weak to withstand the negative effects of external economic change, political disturbances or natural events. In terms of the Irish famine, the successive failure of the potato crop was economically devastating. However, this came on the heels of severe price fluctuations and the damage to the Irish cottage industry as a result of developments in the textile industry.

Present day Third World economies have suffered similar setbacks. Somalia's pastoral economy, which is based on barter between nomadic herders and small farmers, was devastated by the economic and political turmoil which the country suffered from the mid-1970s onward. International Monetary Fund (IMF) policies which were implemented in the early 1980s undermined the pastoral economy and Somalia's dependence on imported grain increased. Local farmers were displaced from their lands and people's consumption patterns changed from the traditional maize and sorghum to imported wheat and rice. Currency devaluations and the switch to cash crops by large farmers further undermined the capacity of local people to acquire food. When hit by drought and civil war in the late 1980s, famine was inevitable.

The problem of economic underdevelopment is a major factor in food insecurity. In nineteenth century Ireland government neglect of future development initiatives and the failure of landlords and tenants to make land improvements left the people extremely vulnerable to political or natural adversity. The poorest simply did not have the resources to invest in their own development. The landlords and others who did have the means lacked the enthusiasm for investment in agriculture, fisheries, transportation and manufacturing due to absenteeism and the high level of rural unrest and violence. A similar situation is present today in many under-developed countries.

Many sub-Saharan African countries have been impeded by a lack of effective foreign and local investment in their economies. Decades of civil war in Sudan and Angola have hindered foreign investment and the development of indigenous production and markets. More seriously, this underdevelopment has led to a dependence on outside

assistance which further damages local capacities for self-help
and growth.

It is a fact that famine is often caused, not by a collapse in
food production but by a collapse in the economic capacity of
people to acquire food. As a result, efforts to eradicate famine
must be targeted more toward the long-term development of
people's ability to access food and other resources than to
merely providing short-term relief.

War has been an important part of many famines. When
foreign powers fuel conflicts through military and financial
assistance the results can be catastrophic. Such support
enables dictatorial regimes to repress democratic dissent,
silence the media and to deny human rights. The war effort
becomes all important and even the most basic human right to
life is ignored. Part of the task then of preventing or tackling
the horror of famine is political advocacy for democratic
governance which includes the active involvement of civil
society and with it respect for human rights and in particular
for freedom of expression. Indeed, no major famine has
occurred in a properly functioning democracy with a free press
and free movement of people.[30]

Countries which have made significant strides in some areas
on respect for human rights such as the UK and France are
also major exporters of arms. In comparison the resources set
aside for development efforts pale into insignificance while the
money spent on arms purchases by some of the world's poorest
countries is obscene. The 1998 *Human Development Report*
points out that global military spending is $780 billion or 60
times the estimated additional annual cost of achieving
universal access to basic health care and adequate nutrition in
all developing countries which totals $13 billion. Challenging

---

30 At the same time such conditions do not mean that a famine will not occur. For
example a democratic government without adequate resources at a time of food
shortage and without access to external assistance to make up the shortfall may not be
able to avert famine.

the immorality of the scale of the international arms trade is therefore an important aspect of any strategy to eradicate famine even when the reality of job losses in producing countries has to be faced. Such unemployment is a far lesser evil than oppression and violence against the poor by the parties to military conflicts.[31]

(iv) One of the greatest temptations is for those with power to abuse their authority. There is no greater example of power than to have control of food in the midst of a hungry populace. It is an understandable temptation to use this power to further political, social and religious goals but it is as morally reprehensible as it is politically attractive. We have already analysed the extraordinary effect of "souperism" on Irish Catholic consciousness during the Great Hunger. Difficult as it is to believe the practice of exchanging food in order to recruit new adherents continues today. African Rights reported from Sudan in 1997:

> Providing an education for non-Moslem children can be the first stage in a process of conversion to Islam. One example of this comes from the Nuba Mountains, where the government uses offers of food and clothes to lure rural children to schools in government-controlled towns. One escapee from the towns reported: "For those children staying in Um Dorein and al Atmur (peace camps), now they have schools for them. These are khalwas, and they are only taught Arabic and the Koran. At the beginning, the parents of children refused to allow them to go to the school, because they were only Islamic

---

31 While job losses would result in the short-run it is also worth noting that if the same amount of resources invested in the arms industry were invested in other sectors many jobs would be provided.

schools, but the authorities decided to cook zelabiya (cake/bread) for them, and also provide tea, so the children began to go of their own accord."[32]

That this grotesque practice still continues is a sad indictment of humanity. Those who continue to participate in it might learn an important lesson from the Irish famine: victims of hunger are slow to forget those who sought to rob them of their culture and traditions because they were hungry. Such proselytism is morally indefensible.

The manipulation of food for political and military ends is equally disturbing. In situations of crisis, relief food can become part of power structures and power struggles. In Sudan, Somalia, Angola, Mozambique amongst others, politicians and armies have caused food crises and blocked and directed for their own ends relief programmes which target civilians. A longstanding Sudanese partner of Trócaire's, Bishop Macram Max commented recently:

> In war-torn Southern Sudan, food is being used as a weapon against the civilian population. Tens, if not hundreds of thousands, of innocent citizens have died as a result of the government withholding food from them, including relief food provided by the international community.

Effective famine prevention demands that we challenge traditional philanthropic and technocratic procedures and instead locate the challenge of hunger in the political and economic arena. Issues of land reform, ownership of natural resources, participatory development, conflict resolution, distribution of economic resources and the role of governments

---

32 African Rights, *Food and Power in Sudan*, London, 1997, pp. 222-23

in famine prevention are central to the achievement of food security. These were pertinent issues in Ireland 150 years ago. The Christian challenge today is to ensure that these issues remain on the agenda and that we continue to pursue them in the search for justice for all.

3 Proclaiming the reign of God

Almost 2,000 years ago Jesus of Nazareth spoke of the reign of God as healing for the sick, hearing for the deaf, new sight for the blind, freedom for prisoners, good news for the poor and bread for the hungry.[33] Before we can really appreciate the meaning of healing, hearing, new sight, freedom, good news and bread we need to become aware of the realities of sickness, blindness, deafness, prison, poverty and hunger. Only when we immerse ourselves in these human experiences can we discover who Jesus really was, for his ministry was all about lifting burdens. Whether the burdens were created by a scrupulously strict religious sensibility or blind obedience or political corruption or grinding poverty or sickness or lack of self-esteem or pride or prejudice, the result was the same: people were in need of healing. The meaning of the miracle stories in the Gospels is not that Jesus was some sort of esoteric magician who could solve all of life's most inscrutable problems, but rather that he was one who brought healing and hope into the most abject human situations.

The world is full of evil. Unless one lives a completely blinkered egocentric existence the pain of human experience is all too obvious to see. In facing this reality we can turn our backs in despair or throw our hands in the air at the futility of human life. But the call of Christian discipleship demands otherwise. It demands that we always seek to lift the burden. Whether this means helping people to stand up and walk on their own, or exorcising their fear of the unknown, or exploding their minds through education, or feeding them when they are too weak to feed themselves, or opening their eyes to the reality of life, or challenging them to let go of hurts and prejudice, or liberating those who are unjustly oppressed, or

---

33 The meaning of the term kingdom or reign of God in Jesus' ministry is analysed in depth in Albert Nolan, *Jesus Before Christianity*, London, Darton Longman and Todd, 1977; Eamonn Bredin, *Disturbing the Peace*, Dublin, Columba Press, 1985 and Dermot A. Lane, *Christ at the Centre*, Dublin, Veritas, 1990.

introducing them to ever greater horizons of transcendence and beauty, or unsealing their ears to hear the divine echo in their hearts, or unleashing their hope for the future, or sowing the seeds of eternal life, the healing ministry of Jesus is continued as "the blind see again, the lame walk, lepers are cleansed, and the deaf hear, the dead are raised to life, the Good News is proclaimed to the poor" (Luke 7:22). Once a person receives the gift of healing then the possibility arises of moving on without the crutch or the grudge or the closed mind, whilst the future is no longer dictated by forces outside the individual but becomes an invitation to personal fulfilment. It is unquestionably true to say that the most important reality in Christian discipleship is healing. In the Gospels healing occurs through the spoken word and through the laying on of hands. The human word of kindness, compassion and justice can indeed heal but too often our words wreak havoc in their bitterness, apathy and prejudice. Similarly if we are to lay our hands in healing then we will have to lift our hands to help.

The horror of famine is a burden that Christians must seek to lift. They do so in the hope that those who suffer such a calamity might be enabled to take hold of their future so as to create the social, political, economic and agricultural conditions in which the causes of famine can be addressed. But the realities of the market place often hinder such progress. Christians must be challenged to face the fact that whole communities can be condemned to never ending cycles of hunger and degradation. When this is the case the proclamation of the reign of God demands that certain realities be named and addressed. Among these one would include the following:

(a) Donor accountability
Government and non-governmental agencies which provide aid must be held accountable for their actions. Aid which only increases the dependency of recipients on donor nations is a

modern form of colonialism. When communities or nations become dependent on outsiders either for food or for the means to produce food they have become little more than slaves. On the twenty-first anniversary of the foundation of Trócaire, the Irish bishops stated:

> The delivery of financial and emergency assistance to the developing countries is not enough. What is also required is a political response from governments aimed at solving the deep structural problems which underlie world poverty.[34]

Famine relief and development aid are meant to liberate peoples rather than to subject them to new forms of slavery. The ultimate sign that the values of the reign of God are beginning to supplant the values of the rich and powerful will be when there is a serious shift in terms of resource flows from poorer Southern countries to the wealthy nations of the North. According to the World Bank Global Development Finance, total sub-Saharan African debt in 1997 was $222.6 billion and annual debt repayments (interest and principal) were $12.6 billion. Yet UNICEF has estimated that $9 billion would cover the additional annual costs of meeting basic health, nutrition and education needs for the whole population of Sub-Saharan Africa.[35]

---

34 Pastoral Letter of the Bishops of Ireland on the 21st Anniversary of the founding of Trócaire, March 1994.
35 *Human Development Report 1996*, United Nations Development Programme/ Oxford University Press, p. 73. As the figures are for different years an appropriate amount should be added on for inflation. However, the statistics highlight the opportunity cost of resources being channelled into debt repayments as opposed to meeting basic needs. See also Trócaire North South Issues Paper No. 21 - *Towards a Human Development Approach to Debt Sustainability* by Henry Northover, Karen Joyner and David Woodword for an alternative approach to measuring debt sustainability. The authors point to the need to set aside resources for basic needs first and to take into account a country's revenue base. They conclude by noting that under this alternative measure 10 countries, including Rwanda, Mozambique, Ethiopia and Tanzania would qualify for 100% cancellation.

In the meantime those who administer aid should be made accountable, both to their donors and to the recipients of aid, so that this very aid does not itself simply bolster the coffers of the rich and powerful nor damage local capacities for production, nor impede development. Aid agencies also have an obligation to highlight instances of damaging global trade policies which undermine the benefits of aid and to draw attention to human rights abuses and structural corruption so that these do not become entrenched in the mode of charity as a response to famine.

(b) The dignity of those who are hungry
Famine robs victims of their dignity and often their lives. The manner in which these victims are represented by the western media and relief agencies is often deeply disturbing. Although the picture of an emaciated person or a corpse may stir those who see the representation to donate monies, the question of the dignity of those who are hungry must be addressed. Is compassion without the development of a deeper understanding of what is happening of any real value? All images that intend to awaken a sense of compassion should also provoke the observer to delve further into the relevant issues. Otherwise there is a real danger that such images will simply confirm well established stereotypes: that famine is inevitable, that it is natural, that Africans need others to feed them, that the victims are incapable of doing anything for themselves. The truth is somewhat different: famine is never inevitable as those with power can always take steps to avoid it; famine is seldom if ever the result of natural disasters - political and economic forces are the major causes; the people of Africa are traditionally self-sufficient and the victims of famine make the most extraordinary efforts to help themselves, and others, even in the midst of great suffering. In her book on this topic, Margaret Kelleher comments:

Simplistic and shocking images are sometimes defended because of their claimed affective power, their ability to "move" the spectator, and, more specifically, to generate financial donations. Their role is thus, as one commentator has sardonically observed, to "nourish western appetites for charity"...

The political consequences of these images should not be underestimated... On the part of the spectator, they promote a fatalism regarding what is seen: people's hunger emerges as somehow inevitable. The function which may be played by female images is particularly significant in this regard. Scenes of women unable to feed their children, of a child suckling at the dry breast of its mother or a despairing mother holding her dead child, are chosen to convey the breakdown in a primary or "natural" order... The resulting implication, that famine is a natural rather than a political or economic event, is itself a political message, regrettable but also convenient.[36]

To believe that mother earth is responsible for famine is to revert to a very primitive form of religious belief. To believe in the reign of God proclaimed by Jesus of Nazareth demands that we try to understand and interpret our world, not least in terms of our responsibilities towards others. In this context our compassion must not rob others of their dignity.

(c) The idolatry of market forces
The market is not amoral. At times the effects of market forces are undeniably immoral. This is not surprising when one considers that if the market operates without any regulation then the weakest of the weak are simply abandoned. There is

---

36 Margaret Kelleher, *The Feminization of Famine*, Cork University Press, 1997, pp. 228-9.

no better example of this than the export of food from famine-stricken countries. Such incidents, in the Irish and other famines, are well recorded:

> The famine years witnessed the terrible irony of thousands of peasants starving to death while ships laden with wheat, barley, oats and livestock left Ireland for England. Similar scenes have occurred in more recent times. When Chad was suffering the effects of famine in the mid-1980s large quantities of food were being exported to Cameroon and Nigeria where more favourable food prices were to be found.[37]

Other examples of exporting food during famine include Bangladesh in 1974, parts of Kenya in 1979-80, Ethiopia in 1984-85 and Sudan in 1989. It is not surprising that producers want the highest price possible for their goods but it offends every fibre of human decency to export food for greater profit from countries where the indigenous population is hungry. The issue of hoarding food in times of shortage, whether for personal use or in the hope of economic gain when market pressures increase its value, is relevant here too. If ever one wanted evidence of the worship of the false god of the market then this is surely it. The value systems which justify such actions are manifest in other spheres of the food market as well. Look, for example, at the wholesale destruction of crops and livestock in western countries in order to guarantee the prices that producers receive. The "dumping" of heavily subsidised European beef and other agricultural products on Third World markets and the negative effects this has on local small farmers and industries is inherently unfair. The emergence of hyper-intensive agriculture raises crucial questions that we are only beginning to debate. In this debate

---

37 Sinead Tynan, *Famine in Ireland and Overseas*, Trócaire, 1995, p. 9.

the proclamation of the reign of God will demand that the worship of false gods be named and rejected.

(d) The temptation to despair and violence
In attempting to address all of these issues it will often appear that the task is simply too great and then we face the greatest temptation of all, despair. The final intercession of the Our Father is "lead us not into temptation but deliver us from evil". The temptations to which Jesus was referring were not just some whims or attachments in our own lives but the temptation to lose faith when faced with the ultimate tragedies and evil that unfolds before us. Inevitably we will loose faith if we trust only in ourselves for it will become all too obvious that we cannot solve the problems of the world. Christians believe that God is active in history and that God's reign is encountered in healing, reconciliation and liberation. Throughout this century Christians have spoken of building this kingdom or reign of God. But this is the first and last temptation - to believe that we humans are God. One of the most insightful religious thinkers of the century, the Swiss Calvinist theologian Karl Barth, vehemently rejected terms like "building God's kingdom"; the task of human beings is not to act as if they are God but rather to witness to the values of God's reign as revealed in the life of Jesus of Nazareth. In witnessing to these values Christians will become aware that they cannot do everything but that we can always do something to lift the burdens that oppress ourselves and others. To believe that we must solve all of life's problems will induce total paralysis; when this burden is taken from our shoulders then we can begin to do something about the realities that bear down on others. One of the greatest of these painful realities is famine and its results. Those who suffer famine and its terrible consequences are in need of healing. When we human beings attempt to heal the wounds of life we are truly witnessing to God's reign in our midst.

In confronting the terrible evils and intolerable suffering that have resulted directly from human action it is not surprising that the oppressed have often turned to violence to protect themselves. The temptation for the best of people to turn to violence in order to change unjust structures is enormous. Down through history this has happened over and over again. It is a particularly painful issue for committed Christians; at various times throughout history Christians have turned to violence as the only alternative, some even to the point of the final act of self-sacrifice. Those who have never had to face the radical injustices and horrible events that lead to the taking up of arms should be slow to judge those who have done so in good conscience. Listen to some words from the 1840s again. Bishop Maginn of Derry said,

> For myself, as a Christian bishop, living as I am amidst scenes that must rend the heart of any having the least feeling of humanity, though attached to our Queen... I don't hesitate to say to you that there is no means under heaven that I would not cheerfully resort to redeem my people from their present misery; and sooner than allow it to continue, like the Archbishop of Milan, I would rather grasp the cross and the green flag of Ireland and rescue my country, or perish with its people.[38]

Rousing words like these were quite common on the lips of priests in late 1847 and into 1848. Owen O'Sullivan, the parish priest of Killorglin, wondered aloud at a repeal meeting in Killarney if armed resistance was not necessary.

> Seek the answer from the millions of our poor countrymen who are rotting in their graves because of the misrule of England... if their constitutional appeal (were) treated with ridicule, he for one... was prepared to take his stand with the people.[39]

---

38 Quoted in Donal A. Kerr, op. cit., pp. 134-5.
39 Reported in *The Nation*, 22 April 1848.

In the terrible autumn of 1847 violence did indeed break out, though it was very sporadic. By far the most famous case was the assassination of Major Denis Mahon in Strokestown, County Roscommon. The murder became sensational national news in England when leading Catholic peers blamed the local parish priest Michael McDermott for inciting the killers from the pulpit. He vehemently denied the charge but said that the crime was the result of

the infamous... cruelties which were wantonly exercised... against a tenantry, whose feelings were already wound up to woeful and vengeful exasperation, by the loss of their exiled relatives, as well as by hunger and pestilence.[40]

When the victims resort to violence the great moral dilemma always arises: why create more victims? For experience suggests that this is what violence always does. The people around Strokestown were the crippled victims of famine and the eviction policy of Major Mahon. That some of them resorted to violence is hardly surprising but it still does not settle the moral quandary that such actions pose. All across Europe people revolted in 1848 against foreign domination and social exclusion but events in Europe turned the Irish clergy and many others against violence as it brought back the memory of the terrible bloodletting of 1798 and the futile suffering that resulted. The death of the radical Archbishop of Paris, Denys-Auguste Affre, while attempting to mediate on the barricades in 1848 sent shock waves across much of Catholic Europe. The death of one who supported many of the goals of the revolutionaries seemed to demonstrate again the futility of violence. Right down to today this remains a great moral question - surely violence is a useless response to the reality of victimhood since it creates more victims?

---

40 *Freeman's Journal*, 10 December 1847.

(e) Liberation theology

If people are to overcome the temptation to violence then political action must be both possible and effective. It is imperative for Christians to involve themselves in the task of building communities founded on justice and compassion. This is a political task. It has led to contorted debates in the Catholic Church especially concerning the role of clergy. For centuries priests have been banned by canon law from involvement in party politics but some have found it impossible not to do so. Outstanding examples like Luigi Sturzo in Italy, Michael O'Flanagan in Ireland, Ernesto Cardenal in Nicaragua and Jean-Bertrand Aristide in Haiti clearly felt in conscience that they had to involve themselves directly in politics if they were to fulfil their priestly ministry. Inevitably a serious conflict arises with the Church authorities over the infringement of canon law. Whatever one's perception of the canonical prohibition on priestly involvement in party politics one should have no doubt about the challenge posed by the Second Vatican Council to non-ordained Catholics to involve themselves actively and effectively in the political arena. It was this social awareness at Vatican II that facilitated the emergence of what has become known as liberation theology.

When the bishops and theologians of Latin America returned home after the Second Vatican Council they did so with a renewed sense of the role of the Church in dealing with economic oppression and political tyranny. This led over the ensuing ten years to the evolution of a new liberation-oriented theology.[41] No longer would theology be dominated by stuffy lecture halls, antiquated academics, inaccessible ideas or distant libraries but it would be reclaimed by the believing

---

41 Two of the key early works in liberation theology were Gustavo Gutierrez, A Theology of Liberation, New York, Orbis Books, 1972 and Juan Luis Segundo, The Liberation of Theology, New York, Orbis Books, 1976. Many of the central essays and documents that have contributed to the evolution of this theology are gathered in Alfred T. Hennelly ed., Liberation Theology: A Documentary History, New York, Orbis Books, 1992.

community as reflection upon their own lived experience. Liberation theologians are very critical of what they perceive to be the academic irrelevance and the oppressive tone of much of traditional theology. This, they believe, is in large part due to the method deployed. Theologians have traditionally approached questions concerning God, Jesus of Nazareth, justice, poverty, the interpretation of scripture, Church and sacrament in a detached academic manner rather than from the perspective of lived human experience. The human experience that the liberation theologians want to emphasise is that of poverty and social exclusion. The words God, crucified, grace, redemption, saviour, sin, sacrament are interpreted differently depending on the context in which they are spoken and heard; they are spoken and heard in very different ways in an academic lecture hall in Europe than in the midst of famine in an impoverished country. The perspective of the marginalised and socially excluded is critically important for liberation theology as it insists that Jesus of Nazareth made an option for the poor in his proclamation of the reign of God and that his disciples must do the same if they are to interpret authentically his message for later generations. Only from this perspective can one encounter anew the liberating power of the Gospel and the extraordinary responsibility it places on those who seek to take its demands seriously. The Gospel is all about liberating people from that which oppresses them. For liberation theologians the great questions of our time are posed by hunger, poverty, victimisation and social exclusion. These are the burdens that Christians must seek to lift today.

The liberation theologians are definitely correct in much of what they have to say: that salvation is properly understood as liberation from that which oppresses humanity, that Jesus made an option for the poor and that the Church must do the same, that many social and political structures are violently sinful, that such violent structures exclude the majority of the world's population from sharing in the resources of the planet, that ideology so infiltrates institutions that it is difficult to ascertain the truth, that power rests in the hands of the wealthy, that witnessing to the values of the reign of God is the only reason why the Church exists, that such witnessing will mean challenging the structures and power brokers which hold so many in bondage. The Vatican acknowledged these important elements of liberation theology in the dialogue that it initiated in the 1980s but it was also very critical of the perceived use made of Marxist thought.[42] Given that the present Pope lived much of his life under an oppressive communist regime this is hardly surprising. The criticisms that the Vatican made of Latin American liberation theology carry a lot of weight: that any authentic reading of Marx demonstrates his rejection of religious belief, that the only Marxist interpretation of history is class struggle leading to revolution, that Marx did not believe in any spiritual force at work in history, that dialectical materialism is inimical to Christian belief and that the emphasis on social sin risks robbing individuals of a real sense of personal responsibility for their actions.

Many liberation theologians reject these criticisms on the basis that they simply do not apply to their work. However the use of Marxist categories will always be controversial because it leads rather inevitably to the conclusion that the only authentic model of Christian discipleship is left-wing political activism leading to the overthrow of existing power structures. To Christians who suffered greatly under the Marxist-Leninist regimes in Eastern Europe such claims sound at best silly or at worst grossly offensive to the memory of the millions who died at the hands of totalitarian communist regimes. It is false to

---

42 The Vatican looked at important issues in two documents; the first is critical of many trends in liberation theology while the second is an effort to actually construct such a theology. See Congregation for the Doctrine of the Faith, *Instruction on Certain Aspects of the 'Theology of Liberation'*, Vatican City, 1984 and *Instruction on Christian Freedom and Liberation*, Vatican City, 1986. One of the most significant critiques of liberation theology is Michael Novak, *Will It Liberate? Questions About Liberation Theology*, Mahwah, New Jersey, Paulist Press, 1986.

limit Christian discipleship to particular forms of political allegiance but it is absolutely necessary to demonstrate the links between Jesus' proclamation of the reign of God and the liberation of human beings from all that keeps them in bondage, not just at the personal level but also in their social, economic and political lives. A great debt of gratitude is owed to the liberation theologians who have begun the process of conscientising believers to the social demands of the Gospel.

Proclaiming the good news of God's reign today means much the same thing as it did in the time of Jesus: bringing healing and liberation into the lives of those who are oppressed and burdened by life. In attempting to deal with the colossal burdens created by economic and political forces we find no easy applicable blueprint in the Bible. As a result it is perfectly legitimate that one finds Christians scattered across a broad spectrum of political beliefs and allegiances. But if in the scriptures we do not have any macro-economic theory we most definitely have a series of values by which we are called to live. Christians can legitimately disagree on political action but not on basic values. The most basic value of all is our responsibility to others, an awareness that life is not just centred on the individual. Acting on this principle will form one's conscience with regard to personal, social and political life. Failure to live in accord with such basic values will silence the voice of one's conscience and ultimately sever one's links with others.

This is one of the great temptations of life in the western world today - the attraction of privatism. Whatever the merits of privatisation in the politico-economic world, it is a fatal force when it comes to Christian commitment as it empties decisions of their communal implications. Christians can be in good conscience as capitalists or communists or anything else in between but the really important point is that they must be in good conscience and not wallowing in apathy or self-interest, in anarchy or boredom. A good conscience might well make erroneous judgments in complete sincerity; a conscience silenced by apathy and self-interest is almost always insincere. As long ago as the eighth century before Christ, Amos, the lowly shepherd of Tekoa who lived in a time of economic prosperity, prophesied that the silent consciences of those who rip off the poor would eventually lead to disaster since Yahweh would never forget what had happened.

> Trouble for those who turn justice into wormwood, throwing integrity to the ground; who hate the man dispensing justice at the city gate and detest those who speak with honesty. Well then, since you have trampled on the poor man, extorting levies on his wheat - those houses you have built of dressed stone, you will never live in them; and those precious vineyards you have planted, you will never drink their wine.... Seek good and not evil so that you may live, and that Yahweh, God of Sabaoth, may really be with you as you claim he is. Hate evil, love good, maintain justice at the city gate, and it may be that Yahweh, God of Sabaoth, will take pity on the remnant of Joseph....

> Listen to this, you who trample on the needy and try to suppress the poor people of the country, you who say, "When will New Moon be over so that we can sell our corn, and sabbath, so that we can market our wheat? Then by lowering the bushel, raising the shekel, by swindling and tampering with the scales, we can buy up the poor for money, and the needy for a pair of sandals, and get a price even for the sweepings of the wheat." Yahweh swears it by the pride of Jacob, "Never will I forget a single thing you have done".
>
> Amos 5:7-11, 14-15; 8:4-7

4 Conclusion

Celebrating the eucharist

The very origins of Christian belief are found around the table of the eucharist, the source and summit of Christian living. But from the very beginning problems arose about who should be admitted to the eucharistic table. Was the eucharist for Jews only or could those of gentile birth also attend the breaking of the bread? This was the first great crisis faced by the church and it almost tore it apart in the initial decades of its existence. The community in Jerusalem (called "followers of the Way" or "Nazarenes") was naturally attached to the rituals and traditions of the Jews whilst the newly emerging communities in Antioch (where the disciples were first called "Christians") and elsewhere welcomed non-Jews to the waters of baptism and to the Lord's supper. Throughout the late 30s and 40s of the first century relations between Jerusalem and Antioch deteriorated. The arch-conservative James, called the brother of the Lord, was the leader of the Jerusalem community, while Paul was the primary figure in many of the churches that opened their doors to the gentiles. There was a real danger of schism between these Pauline communities and Jerusalem. But in or around the years 46-48 AD an event of crucial significance occurred: famine struck the Roman Empire. It was during the reign of the Emperor Claudius and the small impoverished Christian community in Jerusalem was in dire need. Paul organised a collection for those in Jerusalem (see Acts of the Apostles 11:27-30) and further collections for their relief were made later (see Romans 15:26-28 and 2 Corinthians 8-9). It is ironic that the reality of famine gradually brought these Christian communities closer together so that eventually they could share the bread of the eucharist around the same table. Though it is little known and seldom reflected upon, the relief of famine played a very important part in the emergence of Christianity.

The early believers spoke of recognising the Lord in the breaking of bread. As they did so they would also have to learn how to recognise him in the brokenness of life. But as ever humans were tempted to close their eyes to the suffering around them while being utterly preoccupied with the details of ritual. There was a strong prophetic tradition amongst the Jews that was highly critical of such hypocrisy. No doubt it was a tradition that helped form Jesus' critique of empty ritualism. The prophet Amos wrote: "Let me have no more of the din of your chanting, no more of your strumming on harps. But let justice flow like water, and integrity like an unfailing stream." Amos 5:23-24

And in the prophet Isaiah we find the words:

Bring me your worthless offerings no more, the smoke of them fills me with disgust. New moons, sabbaths, assemblies - I cannot endure festival and solemnity. Cease to do evil. Learn to do good, search for justice, help the oppressed, be just to the orphan, plead for the widow. Isaiah 1:13, 16b-17

Is not this the sort of fast that pleases me - it is the Lord Yahweh who speaks - to break unjust fetters and undo the thongs of the yoke, to let the oppressed go free, and break every yoke, to share your bread with the hungry, and shelter the homeless poor, to clothe the man you see to be naked and not turn from your own kin? Then will your light shine like the dawn and your wound be quickly healed over. Your integrity will go before you and the glory of Yahweh behind you. Isaiah 58:6-8

These words of the Jewish prophetic tradition echo throughout the history of religious belief. They are particularly apposite with regard to Christianity for it is scandalous to share spiritual food while closing one's eyes to the reality of actual hunger.

Bread and wine are amongst the most wonderful of human creations. But they are human creations - they do not grow on trees. From sowing the seeds and tending the vine, to the harvesting of wheat grain and grape, to the sharing of bread and the pouring of wine, human community is created and fostered. Through the work of human hands the fruit of the earth becomes our food and drink. The transformation of bread and wine in the eucharist into the body and blood of Christ is a sign and a foretaste of the destiny of all reality. It is not just we as individuals but the whole of the social and material world that will be transformed into the new creation. As bread and wine already take on the form of Christ so must the social world be configured to the mystery of Christ in anticipation of its final fulfilment. Since sharing in God's own life is our destiny we must humanise the world here and now. Christians are called to work with adherents of all faiths and of none to build a world of human justice and dignity. In the same way as with our hands we create bread and wine so must we struggle with political ideas and institutions to create a humane world. Without such human creativity there would be no eucharist and without eucharist we could die of spiritual hunger.

The eucharist should be a counter-sign to the dominant values of our culture. The contradictions between the spirit of the world and the spirit of Christ should be incarnated in our eucharistic gatherings. The spirit of the world suggests that there are no such realities as society and community but only individuals who must mind their own patch. The spirit of Christ whispers in our minds and sows the seeds in our hearts of openness to others, of personal responsibility for the world in which we live, of acceptance of what the future might bring, of the invitation to plumb the depths of the inner life which completely transcends fashion and appearances, of forgiveness as the most powerful force in the world, of healing for the sick and the infirm, of maturing towards death as the end of life. This spirit of Christ stirs us to build communities of care and responsibility, to work with those who are oppressed, to seek justice and the provision of basic necessities for all. It is these realities that should be incarnated and celebrated in our eucharistic gatherings.

In this paper we have examined important issues which emerge from an historical and contemporary analysis of famine. All of these point to the need to develop a coherent ethical response to what remains one of the most scandalous of all human realities - that in a world of plenty up to 850 million people are still unable to secure basic food for survival. Christains must answer the call to work with the adherents of other religions, and those of no religious faith, to construct a future where this scandal will cease to exist. This work will demand the development of a renewed ethical vision which emphasises human responsibility, the eradication of poverty, fair play in international trade and global solidarity. Education provides the key to such a future. Without an enlightened pedagogy we are doomed to revisit the past over and over again. In awakening our sensibilities and disturbing our consciences, education can liberate us from our inherited stereotypes to embrace the future with renewed energy and hope.

At times in life we should indeed eat, drink and be merry for there is much to celebrate. Ancient religions developed the festival of the first fruits of the harvest to give thanks for the wonderful gifts of the earth and the miracle of existence. With song and dance, games and play, story and ritual the fertility of the planet was celebrated. We should continue such traditions today for if we fail to acknowledge our dependency on the earth we are very likely to become blind to the reality of famine. In this paper we have analysed different dimensions of the human story of famine. These various strands when woven together might constitute a theology of famine. But one must be careful of terms like this because famine is a deeply scandalous reality, one that subverts our faith in God, in ourselves and in the future. The great Christian commandment is "do this in memory of me". We offer the bread and wine in his memory, we forgive sin in his memory, we lay hands on the sick in his memory, we give of ourselves to each other in his memory. We do all of this in anticipation of the end, of the final nuptial banquet where all will have their fill to eat and our hearts will be merry with the new wine of God's kingdom. In the meantime it is a betrayal of Christ's memory not to open our eyes to the realities that oppress so many. In subverting our cosy certainties about who we are and what we are called to be, Trócaire can play a crucial role in the life of our Church.

There is much misery and the people are in a deplorable condition. But this is not all. Lord de Freyne is still carrying out his exterminating systems. He has lately visited several houses and served several processes of ejectment. Kilfree is now a plague spot and were it not for the immense aid which the zealous and tiredless P.P. Rev. Peter Brennan is able to afford, the distress at present prevailing would have been multiplied ten fold. There is no parish in the country that requires more aid than Kilfree. It is remote from any town. It is destitute of local gentry. It is oppressed by absentee landlords and its unhappy people are reduced to the lowest ebb of human suffering.

The Sligo Champion, 29 June 1847